Xing

poems by **Debora Kuan**

saturnalia books

Distributed by University Press of New England
Hanover and London

Saturnalia Books
105 Woodside Rd.
Ardmore, PA 19003
info@saturnaliabooks.com

ISBN: 978-0-9833686-1-8
Library of Congress Control Number: 2011934349

Book Design by Saturnalia Books
Printing by The Prolific Group, Canada

Cover Art: Letha Wilson, "Prism-Pyramid" (2009).
Author Photo: Robert Bettendorf.

Distributed by:
University Press of New England
1 Court Street
Lebanon, NH 03766
800-421-1561

My thanks to the editors of the publications in which these poems, or versions of these poems, first appeared:

"Fortuna" in *Hannah*

"Glacier" in *New American Writing*

"Snug Guns" in *Court Green*

"Noc/Turne," "How to Take Black-and-White Pictures," "Confessions of Porcelain Animals" on Reading Between A & B

"We Shall Sit in the Earth and Watch the Performance," "Anthology of Cyclops," "Assemblage" in *Dragonfire*

"Year of the Beetle" in *Indiana Review*

"Awaken, Yellow Chamber" in *Conduit*

"Pastoral" and "Mollusk & Evening" in *The Iowa Review*

"Articles of Faith" in *Salt Hill*

"Minority Assignment #7" and "Minority Assignment #8" in *American Letters & Commentary*

"R.S.V.P." in *Boston Review*

"Dream of Sabine" (originally "For Jules and Jim") in *Fence*

"The (Pillow) Sham Theory" in *CROWD*

My gratitude and thanks to: Hu, Jenny, and Christine Kuan; Matt McLean; Letha Wilson; Robert Bettendorf; Henry Israeli and Saturnalia Books; my teachers—Mark Levine, Cole Swensen, Emily Wilson, Dean Young, Robert Hass, Arthur Sze, Yusef Komunyakaa, and Jonathan Galassi; my friends and fellow poets G.C. Waldrep and Crystal Curry; the CUNY Writers' Institute; the University of Iowa Writers' Workshop; the Bread Loaf Writers' Conference; the U.S. Fulbright program; and the NJ Governor's School for the Arts.

Table of Contents

for my family

XING, n. crossing, abbreviated (used esp. on road signs).

cross, *n.*, *v.*, *adj.*
1. a mark resembling a cross, usually an X, made instead of a signature by a person unable to write. 2. the Cross, the cross upon which Jesus died. 3. the Cross as a symbol of Christianity. 4. an opposition; thwarting; frustration. 5. any misfortune; trouble. 6. a crossing of animals or plants; a mixing of breeds. 7. a person or thing that is intermediate in character between two others. 8. a crossing. 9. a place of crossing.

xing, *v.* 行

1. walk; travel. 2. pedestrian crossing. 3. prevail. 4. do; carry out.

We are prisoners of something larger
than our respective stories

          —John Yau, "Double Agent III"

...Is it true that the beyond, that everything beyond is here in this life?

          —André Breton, *Nadja*

Articles of Faith

1

I am Ansaphone, hello. My hair color is henna.
On a scale of one to ten, I am considered highly gregarious,
moderately loyal,
decent, diligent, eager to please.
Please leave me a detailed message after the tone.
I will get back to you as soon as possible—

2

Mother, the other day, when I rested
my hands on your shoulders, they seemed so small.
I wonder how you keep your purse on.
I wonder.
I want you to know
I feel the laying on of hands on my head every night,
I remember the feeling of being underwater
with the missionary's hands holding mine. I know you
have heard the rumor: I knock
stones with other girls' stones. Please
do not worry. I am thinking of you
and Father in separate grain elevators
in Kansas. I am thinking about you both.

3

On my way to the post office, I collide with Uncle Chen.
Uncle, I say, you look so

Uncle Chen today. I like the way you
drape your bright chen, it feels
exquisitely Marxist, and I know you are proud to be uncle.
Your socialist car is appropriately rusted, the doors
no longer shut.
Everywhere the magpies are falling, my wires constrict
around the wrists and ankles.
When will it stop?

4

Mother, you are shrinking, I say.
I do not want to alarm you, but
the mathematics of your body proportions no longer add up.
Mother replies: Do not worry, Daughter.
There is milk in my purse. There is time.
I do not think anything will happen
in the grain elevator. I am reading Kahlil Gibran.

5

Q: Would you please tell the congregation who taught you how to shoot a gun?

A: It was my uncle. He asked me to shoot a few soda cans. My family, we
are all renegades.

Q: Do you have anything else you would like to confess? Have you ever had
homosexual relations with a person of the same sex?

A: No. I have only had homosexual relations with persons of the opposite
sex. I find the following words obscene: tit, cunt, dick, dickwad, bang, balls,
clit. The others I have used. When I was young, my father taught me this
phrase: Chairman Mao is the red sun in our hearts! I can say it in two
languages; this is what it sounds like in Chinese: *Mao Zhu Xi shi wo men xin
zhong de hong yang.*

Q: Do you have a strong testimony that Joseph Smith is the true prophet of the true gospel and that the Book of Mormon is another testament of Jesus Christ?

A: On my eighth birthday, I did not go to church. My Buddhist grandmother hid me in a brown cardigan on her bed. I did not want to go under the water with people watching me, or have hands lain upon my head, or afterwards eat cake. I did not want to wear a white polyester gown and have people see my body through my wet clothes, as I rose from the baptismal font.

Q: What has made you change your mind today?

A: Today I do not mind being wet. Today I want to save others.

Year of the Beetle

In the aftermath, even the detour was boarded up
with screws, and we
were quarantined in church closets
to scratch our new names
on burlap squares with chalk. Mark over
mark over mark. I was Coleoptera now, iridescent
when wet, not to be confused with my sister,
Cleopatra, the lisper, who
tucked her waist-length hair into her gray wool trousers.

Everywhere we looked, dirigibles
blotted out the sky, and we dreamed
of a different war,
perhaps one begun with needles.

Once out, we
stuffed our mouths with what we could:
shreds of gauze, mushroom stalks,
muddy envelopes,
and at night, the daring
among us ventured out to the air crash
to pull jade bracelets off charred wrists.

The rest of us scavenged differently.
A garter belt that had fallen from the sky,
antennae. Elsewhere,
a bit of red thread, a teacup
covered in tar.
We didn't know what for.
We moved with our arms outstretched
and gathered up whatever looked alive.

Pastoral

A hobby-horse appeals—

This is our wooden meadow,
nest-stolen calves, and our painter Chao,
painting from winter, gets her red cap bitten off.
Ahead, a color monthed. Ahead, the start of storing.
My one dumb eye is a hungry eye,
it pushes sheep through it.
Needle and bundle and the start of
flowered dresses. Lin has potted smooth stones in white soil,
and now they have sprouted selves.

Is this anything to paint with?
I have magnetized pearl buttons to other pearl buttons.
I have waited for any bird to call on me.

And for any constellation. And for any flayed forest.

When I return, even the foxes are white.
They have grass on their backs, which is also
snowed. No one remarks.
I have to lie still until
some life kisses me. Until some animal rotates
himself and settles down in ache.
In surrendered awe and curios.

This is a cut glass collection.
And a cabinet of grass.
A statue made of milk and laid on its side.
Chao says *pony*. Lin offers *cervix*,
matrix, *wire*. But we have landed on *silo*.
We are thinking of shapes for ourselves.

And ahead, we can see it,
an X-ray and a child. One tremendous head
and a body in bone.
I cannot help thinking,
A hood pulled over our horse's head to keep it asleep.
And we wait, we wait,
chewing wool to perfection—

To shepherd. To pause. Where things begin grazing.
This is some silo for storing. This is some green.

Mollusk & Evening

After the party, the women folded up their brains neatly
and brought them indoors. The evening
smelled like fresh wounds on ice.
Second-place. Bleached ribbon.

It struck me that I'd seen this movie before.
A white rook. A white queen. Ember eyes.
The hope chest the garden snails got into,
and the gardener whose face kept changing.

*

I came to understand that the world began
with the sudden deportation
of mammals. Departure/arrival board. A redundant gesture.
Irregular people were just like everyone else now.

I found a warm, flattened fork on Bloomington Street
and followed the direction of its tines.
Into wax hands in particular wax gestures.
Into the relics of the insatiable. Into misguided tires.
Zero and one. Scissors and switches.
All of my refusals.

And in the square, the square. The sound of knives
against a seashell. The sound of scripts thumbed open.
Sound of sunken peach-bites.
Sound of blind ocean. Sound of black sound.
Yellow sound.
The peril of not-sound. A tide going out,

on rewind and the sound of
a dead beetle deep in the crevices of the videotape.

I had heard of new rituals, new trash.
I had heard of lightning leaving a woman's body through her heel.

*

Under a child's tongue, a fever climbed.
It was evening again—

Plastic lawn chairs, strewn with plastic animal masks,
beaded with water.

I lay in my bed, trying to imagine
a blind and deaf baby,
but nothing would close all the way.

Anthology of Cyclops

Thunder tears up her sleeve. And one-eyed
cloud, her one eye clouded over
with junk, turns to face
the monks in hailstorm, busy threading beads. One hook
snares a live thing.

And the sun under sun, under layers of fur and skirt—

Dawn. The fog sheep
wake in droves. Crescents
of breath. An overdose.

I am muffled in pillow. In middle plains.
(Son of an ocean. Knife in the eye.)
A key jiggles in lock at the cave entrance.

The monks begin to cart away the weather.
Wan pink squares of light, after wan pink squares of light—
bolts and electrodes, gas and wick—
No one breathes the helium.
No one breathes.

The oasis' madman is still a madman.
And in that oasis, his axes
sprout through like succulents. Like prickly red beards.
Like alarm and fatal map: *You are here*. Red X.

Often, the chewed-up moon will spread her legs and moan.
O sea.
I hear one voice, but two are speaking—

The Silkmaker's Bride

The mulberry sheds its owl-shape.
It is guileless now.
Closed zoo, dark school.
A shawl over each unseen thing
that orbits.
Obits: The worms spin a warm prize.

How can I criticize
the suitor's offer—a fist of silks
dense as a pendant?
How can I not notice
the spot on the wall, lighter than sun?
Something hung there once.

The bridal veil is unusually heavy.
A frostbitten flag.
I have a cowl around my neck,
but it is no twin to kiss.

Such is this family's fortune—used-up
looms,
a harvest of cocoons.

The solitary pedal endeavors:
Its needle's eye sated with thread,
a child's mouth plugged with milk.

Confessions of Porcelain Animals

From out of a sea-pipe or -groove, a child
smiles back. Its one lost eyelash
a miniature seascape (gull-swept wisp
and brine). We fasten its bonnet with new brass pins,
stuff acetaminophen
where its wind-up once was.

At night, the spotted owls loop *jimmy, jimmy, jimmy*.
Their sooty plumage strewn.

We learn by mimicking the inaudible,
the dead eagle now
spread-eagle, the doll's lips slightly
curled in speech.

Now these painted hands and painted feet.
Now the skipping record *Jealousy*   *the dog*
with the transparent   coat.

We learn by rote. By milk and panada and pap.
(In infancy, we sucked a cow's horn.)
—*The child's too weak to be washed.*
—*Then rub it in salt and wine.*

Pharmacopoeia

We made the animal
out of a wooden stool and rolls
of felt and adhesive bandages,
then took it out to the desert
and laid it by a medicine chest
which had lost its knob and mirror.
All around us, waxwings
sated themselves on berries,
huddled together in bushes,
and found themselves unable to fly.
Inside the chest,
little prostheses, rubber,
unlabelled vials. A brush
without its bristles.
A coin, in the event of a question.
Our dismantled valves still
opened and closed, but slower.
We could ride the animal, but not far.
This is the fabric of our inner lives,
laid across a threshold
and glued together with wax.
This is desertion:
a body unravels from its frame.
We came to understand
our place as elsewhere, anywhere,
always just before or after
the shutter snapped itself shut.
We would shuffle off again,
strung with our makeshift bells—
copper funnels tethered to cords—
to clank our cabinet psalms,
to come upon others in sleep,
and with our magnifying glasses
burn holes in other tents.

2

Minority Assignment #2

We sultry the lampshade & suture the lambchop.
We but widows wasp & swap.

We hookline&sinker gin our drink.
We water our bent-up Bible with ink.

We con & thereof canvass.
We nuclearize & notice.

We scrub our oily skins, confess our cardboard sins.
We blunder the pure blood & blame the breast milk.

We but cowl necks, we but fur.
We noose-slip beneath the radar.

We anaesthetize our tribal bones.
We but nuns undo the union.

We capture the culpable bells.
We but soldiers wet ourselves.

We peep & spy & sleeper.
We exoticize our features.

We pry apart our private parts.
We don the nods & pocket the wads.

We hook our masks around our ears.
We prepare our rightful heirs.

Minority Assignment #7

Or, imagine the minority is subjected to a kind of medical examination before going into a war. The examiner puts it through a set of standardized tests. Then, he gives his verdict in the form "So-and-so can throw a spear" or "can throw a boomerang" or "is fit to drive a tank," etc.

Ask yourself: Is there a certain flatness to the foot of the minority? Does it exhibit signs of fatigue, nausea, or fluid retention? Explain.

We say, "Minority will happen," and also, "Minority comes toward me"; we refer to the log as "minority," but also the log's coming toward me.

Therefore, if we see a man with sunken minority, but who has not the use of his minority for some reason or other, we should still say he is a man of qualities.

Did you notice that minority, or did you only say there was one because you think there must be one? When did you know for certain?

A minority opening clockwise is happy and optimistic.

A minority closing counterclockwise is in pain.

A left-handed minority, moving away, is a vanquished enemy.

To Kill a Frog

Blue dusk, pricking icicles, the stench of cuttlefish and bloodstain.

I feel unclean, a woman whispers through the lattice. Give me something. Not an amen to close one's lips on, but a blister of pastel tablets, mint sprigs, yogurt frozen in the fingers of surgical gloves.

The heat rising.

Flicker in a crocus, quelled. I walk into the giant sleeves of a dress and let the ripped seams tickle my shins.

Merciful white birdhouse, swallow this tiny bird—

Prayer: A ladder drops its rungs.

Sly. How you hissed that word once in bed, dragging out its sibilance, brightening the vowel. Meaning the 2 a.m. dinner he and I ate in secret, sitting on the bedroom floor—steamed rice, pickled cabbage, little anchovies the color of chrome. Afterwards, there was nothing to do, but brace ourselves for your return.

Prophecy: The sun in someone's mouth, slipping out by a thread.

Yet it rises.

The woman falls asleep in a tub of cold bathwater.

I dream that I have witnessed through a keyhole: A Mormon bishop unzipping his fat suit from the tip of the forehead to the ankle to reveal another man.

When the missionary immersed me, I resisted. Felt my chest rise up to the surface like a quiet buoy. *I feel like I should tell you, I'm not doing this for the right reason. Also: My right foot broke the surface.*

But it didn't seem to matter. I had been faithful to your lapidary ghost.

A bloom of steam, a fiery vowel.

I dreamed that I could survive the deceptions of clarity. Heat breaking the water's skin. The chronology of belief. A single white dress.

Awaken, Yellow Chamber

At 33, a man grows fat amid the crabgrass. Watch him
dangle his hat from a broken branch.
Watch him dangle, Hang Man.
He is in initials. He is in cahoots
with owls and ghosts, tree tumors, and the river
brimming, nearly flooded over,
brightening, brightening,
yellow.

Follow him to the stuck carousel in the open field.
To all the matrons, all the slow blue cows of daylight.
Consider all the ponds and the roofs they'll bear
in winter. Consider the evensong
and ice. Consider the bloodsuckers on a full-blooded man.

The science of sacrifice is the same anywhere.
Take two objects side by side; ignore their differences.
That *thresh* approaches *thrash* is not beside the point.
There is no sign of life here, but the sound of knocking.
Ulna against radius. Socket to socket.
O your wrist
and what it supplies in ink: time and numbers, a yellowed page.

*

At 33, translucent winters, the beckoning of scrims.
Cain with a hand over his forehead tries to obscure his mark.
That he could be any man is not beside the point.

He sits with a makeshift Ouija under the painted lamp.
Wet bowl on milk-glass tabletop. Feather fingers.
In the afternoon, he eats figs and sesame seeds and waits for a sign.

*

At 33, you will follow any drops
of blood down the boulevard.
To return to a courtyard, to return to a bunker beneath the bridge,
to a yellow chamber draped in yellow voices.

You will hammer through the glass cases of
childhood monarchs pinned by the black of their wings.
You will hum with the jars, wet at the lips, touched by human hands.
And set about to build a tower: mattresses tied together with rope.

Minority Assignment #8

Minority thrashes its long tail against the shore, making its mating call. A minority canyon with minority canon. The inmate sits silently, strapped to a polygraph. Hiccup, sigh, piss, yawn. Minority defied, minority bent. I shuffled a puck up toward minority. Slingshot, slipshod, crockpot space pod. I paddle the ping against the pong. I saddle the alien with cheer. What have you done with my minority wife? One hand up her skirt, the other thumbing her lips—I hear your back-room minority sips. An apple cored of essential minority is ripe for baking, basting, and licking. Private tongue, public authority. She's gagged with minority in a majority coatroom. The bull's-eye wobbles in the nightly minority, counting crickets on curtains and cots. Digging minority on minority plots. Some will call it a pawn-shop hock. Fermented soybeans, clotted white honey. Each time we stop to look for minority, it takes up time and we lose money.

R.S.V.P.

During the winter of 1967, I was working as a laborer for the Department of Sanitation, removing snow from city streets. I held my wedding in a small, but respectable, bomb shelter, which seemed to surprise no one. Did you know this? Vladimir Mayakovsky's brain weighed 1700 grams, against a human average of 1400, when they extracted it from his body. Together we wept. The realization had come too late. Perfect hindsight would have revealed that there was hardly enough oxygen for us to get through our vows in their entirety. In any case, we dared to believe in recycling, immaculate urban landscapes, where guilt comes from. I had been raised a virgin, and my sense was that genuine faith took many forms. What more could anyone hope for? Every day was like walking into a room packed to the ceiling with white feathers choking its sleepers. Nothing meant something to me. To my surprise, I found that my bridegroom still had large pockets of baby fat on his body. As soon as he fell asleep, I would roll over and bite them. Tremendous tears—but real—rolled down my face. He was as beautiful as a little girl. It was February. I woke to the sound of an infinite corridor crowding my bones with awe. I was somebody's wife.

Paolo & Francesca

1

Dear God, I hope all is well back at the institute.
We are at the warehouse
cleaning out the refrigerators
and all the food is on the floor.
I miss you.
The bed is cold at night under the windows
and only the peeping-tom
white birches are willing
to watch me undress.

2

Once I was a fine-haired lamb
eating my breadcrumbs and sugar.
I sang my praises in a treeless field.
Love was a whistle
I played with my mouth.

Then Christ crossed the field.
The sharp summer grass
pricking his weary ankles—
little nicks & hyphens.
Here, spotted cows.
There, fences.

All afternoon, the cloudless August climbed.
And all its cloudless children were its song.

The hands on our heads were our fathers'.
Our underwear was white.

3

Dear God,
Sometimes the lamb is here, curled
like a coarse dark hair on the pillow.
All he desires
is to hold me,
sleepless and mindless and blind.
I let him.
His feet are milky smooth,
and sometimes he kisses mine.

We are teaching each other devotion
like the man and the woman
of the airy white warehouse
roped together at the waist.

Face to face, we are trying to fly.

Pastoral

This is the map of stationary cloud and crow.
Felt bird perched
atop felt world at last,
while the white colts crowd around.
And, in his wagon, Lin sits still,
pulls on his hand-me-down black boots.
Left foot, right foot. All roads end
in spools of pink, then fasten to other roads.

This is the map, and this is its legend.
In far-left field, the cemetery
pinwheels languish in non-spin.
Unshiver, atremor.
The quiet corruptions feel several.
Nameless headstones, loose teeth.
A hand inside a stopped watch,
which cannot feel its gears.

Chao begins another story, the one
about the opaque form
against its opaque field.
Another manifestation of owl.
We go the only way we can: brick by brick,
drum by drum.
We wonder at the flatness of travel, and how
beneath us, against us,
another thing fattens.

So this is exile, this is flight.
Women crossing the landscape in droves,
dropping silverware, gold
heirlooms, hair.

The good hand aids the mangled one.
We doctor. We hold our tongues
and check our mouths for sores.
At night, we wrap a pear in long woolen underwear
and wait for our arrival.

Panorama

Chao's double portraits are always of the same person. Lin sitting in the chair, and Lin standing next to the chair. O homonym. *Ad hominem.* This is one version of memory: The person you dream of is always in duplicate. Or, he swells in size to enormity, lost in layers of sheepskin, and you meet him in blackened cities, as soon as you step out the door.

Look at it another way: One digs a hole to hide the hole the divot made. Around Chao's neck dangles a little necklace of pins pulled from grenades.

Today, I am in the felt tent, sorting scraps. In the street, a sheet metal worker is setting fires.

Snug Guns

One took the place of the horse. Split
ropes, dun hearse, he

dragged the crippled wagon
over a hillock of bees.

The rest of us inside—I, up front—
rode and cocked our guns

against an army of muscle
and hum. Our crepe paper

faces awake.
This is the pine needle

I shoved deep in hand
to remind me of my hand.

Teach me how to swathe myself—
a private binding—

against the arrival of hooves.

A Suitcase of Lightbulbs Gets Left on the Road

When I went to see the apartment, it
was an elevator and quite small,
in the corner, a library attendant at work, tossing all the books.
"You've heard the sound," the chemicals said.
"You will be videotaped,"

It went on and on like that. A thousand planes took off
with sailors and sheriffs. A bit of red,
some song. The fluorescence of bright-eyed children.

In Ecclesiastes:
"A bird of the air shall carry the voice."

So the chemicals carried me everywhere,
clinking their test tubes, making fun.
They pelted brass buttons and batteries at me,
through the groves, along the coast.
I heard laughter in running water.

My mother, the policeman's daughter, stacked the family
in haphazard piles. Did her impressions
of the wind, her barefoot brothers, the yellow mutt.
She might have asked in the war of '49,
"What will *mall* be like?"

A suitcase of dead lightbulbs thrown open on the street.
A horsefly swarming over. A desert.

I hung up some colored bits of string,
circled the dead rhubarb in the yard.
Let it be said now, I was a tenant of the elevator.
I dressed in harsh surgical lights.

Never to think, sirs, *One more thing…*
Never to chance another wilderness.

Apprenticeship of the Marionette

I am sitting on the phonebook, engaged in another conversation with Lin. Notice how he buttons up his sweater wrong, yet nobody points this out. Or how, if he lifts his arm, you can see a huge gaping hole where the seam split at the armpit? I try to bring this up to him, but he says, *Hey, I don't hear anyone complaining.*

From where I am, the day looks flaccid and grey, the shade of leftover oatmeal. I am trying to recall the problem of the room with a pile of sawdust. Not resolve, recall. First, I have to recall it, then I can resolve it. How does it go again? You come upon an empty room, locked from the inside. A man hangs from the ceiling. Beneath him, a pile of sawdust.

My hands float like handkerchiefs in my lap, trying to ascertain their moment.

No, beneath him, a puddle of water. That's an easy one. You know the solution, Lin says, barely even looking at me. He is carving eyes in a new apprentice, his body hunched over a pile of wood shavings.

The Cue Ball & the Seahorse

Certain mornings, we woke to see a seahorse
skeleton pinned to the peeling wallpaper
on our bedroom wall. The sky outside,
a new anatomy.
We would slip on our shoes and go out,
fingers raised in awe
against its conch-like surface:
Apex. Little whorl, little suture,
bigger whorl, bigger suture,
until we reached the aperture.

Meanwhile, last year's cue ball
quietly bloomed in the yard,
and we decided on new expressions,
Dollhouse rots from the head
and *Blue fridge, blue frogs.*
Our mouths burned all winter
with the pleasure of saying them.

But the falconer would not appear,
however my limbs ached
or however the stones in my head
fell in their various rhythms.

Instead, the hole we'd dug in summer
on the edge of our family property
continued to widen with consequence,
and what we could not keep from draining down it
almost took us too.

In January, Lin sent me a postcard
of a hotel swimming pool
to tuck in the edge of my mirror.

I wrote my reply on a piece of dough
painted black
and flattened with my palm,
but the rain got to it first, then the dogs.

We Shall Sit in the Earth and Watch the Performance

1

Preparations for her field concert began early in the day. The mute men rose at dawn to dig the rectangular trench from clover and clod—seen from above, a frame branded in the world, into which the rest of us would settle.

We could make out the aluminum ribcages of the horses, as they reclined in whatever shade they could find. We'd lean sycamore sticks against their bodies and taunt "What will you do?," then disappear behind the dogwoods. Later, as if nothing had happened, we'd crawl back out to feed the beasts of burden tea from pewter spoons.

Once, I was in the house peeling a hard-boiled egg, when I got up and went to the window, lifting its tattered curtain. As I did so, winged things in the yard flinched in unison, and before anyone could utter "Fire!," the dour finches flitted and flapped, and then rose together into the trees, like a blanket of blown ash. The world was sodden, orphaned. When I looked up, I saw Lin sitting on the roof of the house, his hatless head buried in his hands.

2

The player arrived at noon, her hair parted into three sections, a mitten in her mouth, and her instrument tucked beneath her arm. The instrument, which none of us had ever touched, only admired from our trench, was constructed mostly of wood, its top carved with grooves and attached with various metal contraptions and bells, through which she dragged a heavy wire to make music. But it was notorious for its misbehavior. "What do you want from me?" she hissed, while trying to tune it. "What's it going to take?" She wrestled with the side and thrust a chicken bone into one corner. Then, at last, she took her seat in the center of the field-stage.

Everywhere, we were emerging from our houses. We wiped our hands in our aprons and mopped our brows. We nodded at our neighbors. Then we climbed into the trench. Seeds stuffed into the earth. Overhead, the sky was a milky rag about to be wrung dry, as our mother began to sing.

Noc

Is that thing alive? I hear a famisht howl.
—John Berryman, Homage to Mistress Bradstreet

Hush.
Leaking.
We stopper the head with gum wads.

Warn or warm
what elfs one—
bring the brain about and wet it.

Turne

Now we are the headless mannequins. Plainly lain. C minor, autumnal, post-guillotine. We scratch each other's necks.

Concavity as sympathy: the way a beggar shapes his hands. Or, I walk twenty days to meet a phantom pain: a chrome insistence beneath the brow, a steady soreness scrapes the bridge. Far ahead, a lamp-like face. It feigns surprise.

This *is* the other side of glass. A song, trapped in a snuffbox.

What replaces voice: pet cricket, tuning fork, zither placed upon a city wall. Our shoulders slump forward, our palms gesture upward. What has been renewed. Obedience of no nominal value: fermata held indefinitely.

Get in there. Expose (matter): rope and flesh, clef and salt. A tendency to tire.

Light as falsification: my shadow with balloon.

4

Stage Notes from *Clay Winter Wedding*

Costumes

DEATH is a beautiful young man in a blue seersucker suit and cape. His hair, tie, tennis shoes, gestures, and gait are all in the latest fashion. His eyes are like painted dimes in a dime-store's glass case.

His ASSISTANTS, dressed like Rockettes, wear silver leotards, fishnet stockings, and buttoned boots. They trail closely after him, moving in perfect symmetry.

KORA (CHILD) wears tattered overalls, pale make-up, and gold spectacles. Her nose is slightly crooked from a near-fatal accident over a year ago while playing soccer with the lesser gods.

KORA (GROWN) pulls around a small suitcase on wheels, in which to stuff dead flowers. She wears the same gold spectacles, but no overalls; rather, strings of chunky pearls and other gems, elbow-length gloves, a wrinkled veil (under which her hair is tied in a schizoid chignon), and a gown whose tulle hem is frayed and drags apologetically on the stage. Her face is painted as thickly white as a geisha's.

Her mother, CERES, appears only as an authoritative voice projected from the wings. (Or, alternatively, a standard theatrical wind-machine may be used.)

Scenery

A *room* in DEATH's villa. It is an austere room rather like the apartment of a Scandinavian ambassador or logician. In spite of the early light, one suspects that it is surrounded by cold, unfriendly spirits. Funeral meats dress the long dining table. Even familiar objects—e.g., candlesticks, glass paperweights, cutlery, an ant farm, the modest taxidermy on the walls— have a dubious air about them.

In the corner sits a large, cylindrical clay vat, above which is hung a mirror of equal size, positioned so that the audience can see the vat's contents.

Notes on Producing

The *vat* should have a ladder leaning against it, so that KORA can climb into it easily and do her poetic orations. When occupied by any sound, it should produce a sonorous and majestic echo capable of filling the entire theatre.

The *dining table* should be long enough to seat all the assistants, plus DEATH and KORA, comfortably. In fact, it is so long that it falls right off the stage. To the seasoned eye, its surface appears damaged in such a way as to suggest the appearance of being danced upon one too many times.

A *velvet curtain* hides a giant pincushion of a bed.

A *deer's head* over one door is not a symbol for anything. It is a commonplace marker, like true north, around which one might orient oneself when lost.

A *stuffed dove* is poised with beak half-open, as if in song.

Drums and *cymbals* should be used sparingly and only in association with CERES, to drown out her lamentations.

Artifacts from *Clay Winter Wedding*

Dear Kora,

My darling. A rosebud in Eritrea, radiant whistleblower. Without you, the 'cold drums in my ears every morning, a news-like reminder. Your absence is terrifying only because idle strangers conspire to wear your face, to mimic your gestures, to swim toward me in the guise of your body. What can I call this? The theatre of misapprehension. Tapestries in their sad weft and woof. The criss and cross of false missionaries. I remember your voice in clay, its seamless modulations—

Otherwise, I have counted sixteen ants in all, caught between the glass panels. The last inhabitants of the farm hardly recall their former civilization. I, for one, do not care to remind them. There is no blasphemy anymore. There are no duchesses, no dancing. My love, there is not even volition. Our concrete talismans remain in ancestry.

It is difficult to say how my hours are spent. For me to look at a staircase now is to observe that all things move in at least two directions. Follow them. There is something worth discovering. Like Grief, I do not preoccupy myself with inventories. Once when I overturned a cruet of vinegar, I memorized the individual droplets, one by laborious one, as they formed, then fell into a dish—I even learned their names—but I did not count them. That would have been too much.

How long do you think it takes to grind a lens, or inherit a legacy, or overcome hysteria? What would you have chosen if I had never chosen you? This morning, when I woke, I raised my arm to yawn, and the slanted ceiling dismissed me. I heard your faint amusement above. I am sure it was you. Why couldn't I call out to you? Something raw-edged lodged in my throat—

I would never say you must come back, only that you have to. An oration is only as cylindrical as its rhetorical validity. Think of a grain silo. A cork. A lampshade. Somehow artificial light is bearable, because it is easily given, easily extinguished, and no one can possibly expect otherwise.

Death

Dear Death,

What can I say? Life upon returning home is like stepping into a daguerreotype whose faces have all but been rubbed out. I remember loving them, the way one might recall wearing a certain dress, a favorite suit—of diamonds or spades—which now refuses to fit.

You see, I wouldn't ask a gyroscope to remain in torque forever, to spin in perpetuity upon a thread. But like anyone else, I am seduced by the hum. The physics governing a sensuous vibration before friction intervenes. Is not what you call "modulation" really just a schizophrenic ambivalence over head voice and chest voice? Perhaps this is the point.

I sing. The mortar and pestle sing. The buttons and clothespins sing. The bishop, the rook, and the knight sing. Though once we may have reveled in kitsch, we now understand its indulgence. A snowy tree grows out of white bread loaves: the luxury of fluff. Of touch. Of cottony mock-ups of winter—

Of course, there is no two ways about it: I will return. I will gather my skirts, my shreds of freesia and foxglove, my tap shoes and my baton, my Cyrillic and my Swahili, and return to you. After all, what is union without approximation of the other? I cannot pretend to ignore the mimicry of black moths and ashen ones, D sharp and E flat, polish and Polish…

Even I have learned to impersonate you: The beauty of collage is that context is sacrificed to synthesis. Think of découpage. A quilt. A mosaic. I often think I would rather smash apart this world and come away with color than obey its formal purpose and come away with order.

Kora

P.S. I should have expected you would shatter the ant farm after my departure. The tyranny of the queen and her queendom—with its tunnels of air and production—always threatened you so.

Dear Kora,

How it pains me to hear you speak in the rhetoric of gamesmanship! All that comes to mind are castle and checkmate, bluff and flush, ace and trump. Parlor games: the trick devices of boxes within more boxes. One shudders at the thought of such strategies standing between us like magnetic fields we can never penetrate.

Things stand between us, no one denies this. A topography of the rational and irrational. Genealogical trees and Bermuda triangles. Your mother's botanical contrivances look to me, more and more each day, like unwieldy prehistorical flora. I stand speechless in front of its fronds. After all, who can argue with that which predates language? Darling, do not charge me with being one-sided. I remain the same. Things stand between us.

Even between myself and mirrors. It seems to me I see less of my reflection in them now. Is this akin to the photographic blur you find yourself in? A monochromatic hemisphere. The light-sensitive insistence of landscape over location. I cannot say how, just that it is. The staff and dancers are losing patience with me. Picture yours truly: pigeonholed and eating crow. I sniff the scent of mutiny everywhere I go.

What is the diametrical opposite of citizenship? Delinquency? I would rather say abandonment. The heft of an axe through the width of the ply. These are not obligations of gallantry, but vocation. How else can I explain myself to you?

Death

P.S. It was, believe me or not, an accident—admittedly, though, an accident of envy: My world is bereft precisely of the thing that held their civilization intact.

5

Assemblage

for Carrie Gordon, 1955-2003

1

What is one grove
lost? One pod dehisced?
One station of flushed seed, un-
blooming eye?
All morning we are busy dismantling the branches of ash trees,
then stapling them back together
in startling configurations.
A skirt of dead leaves blown open,
a pendulous part, like the wattle of a bird,
or dewlap
flapping in grey eulogy.
We cannot finish affixing,
we come off empty-handed.
All that's left is this small huddle of orchids,
too soft to sink, too meager
for sending—

What is it to carve out the pith,
to falsify a forest, to outlive,
or scratch in gold-leaf *in memoriam*.
What is it
to be de-wintered.

It seems not even mine to mourn you.
No, that belongs to those who washed
your body and held you, swaddled your hairless head,
sang to you as you listened
to a song on the radio, waiting for your heart
to collapse. Those who heard you say
you were happy to go, you
were so happy.
Having been given merely   one hour,
you survived until morning—

3

In class, I am trying to teach Plath
by diphthong,
by coin and moon and siren.
Or else, I say, Notice how she uses *less*:
Eyeless, earless, starless.
Not *blind*. Not *deaf*. Not *the black heap of night*.
But the brutal traces, the shriek
of a missing arm. Strange, unlawful axings.
As if to say,
No bells, but their ringings.
No horses, but their ponderous tracks.
Like the artist Basquiat, I say, going to the blackboard
to cross out the word:
He gives us alchemy, only to take it away.
A chalky line
dragged through the science of gold.
The crossing-
out, which draws us to your absence—

4

Buoyancy. One fleshy grove
repositioned in lumen.
Trees shift their weight
from root to root,
and the sun scratches out its vector,
its sinews repeat in patterns.
Now it is February.
We walk out to the edge of a hairpin,
a blinking needle,
a filament
suspended in pulse.
I sleep fine.
Or too much, dreaming of
enormous atriums, an endless floor showered with eiderdown,
long car-rides with my family into a field of stones.
We bring spades and rags and tulips.
We bow
in synchrony to my mother's count.

Or, we careen on the sea,
our tires barely dipping past the water's surface.
How, sealed in tender immunity,
not a drop seeps through:
exhaust and body somehow
afloat in muscled shadow.

5

Maybe a meadow shorn.
A deposit of fronds and curls,
or finches asleep
in a pillory's holes.

Maybe an acorn splits open
and *that* is de-wintering,
its gnarled meat a calendar
of defiance, stored up in hours.
In fog. In the friable light of condolence.
In this conjuring,
bruised white peaches, shrill alarms.
A makeshift set of leaf.
Tattered head scarves, like plumes,
dress the chill treetops.

So often, I think I see your husband
walking through these brick passageways.
He carries a rolled-up newspaper under his arm,
he is hurrying past. Maybe
he has just seen a war movie,
or is buying some coffee or bread.
He lights a cigarette. It is almost evening.
There are headlights just coming on, children
on roller-skates, touching hands,
on the curb, a leashed
sheepdog waits blind and panting.
And the wind picking up.
I notice the white paint on these walls is chipping.
The bricks missing in places,
a jagged line running through—
And the man crosses the street, and turns a corner,
and passes beyond my view.

6

A circle of crushed berries, nameless
skins, the black mud
stuck in breath—
all these brittle markings,

all these traces,
            tier to tier,
    descend in hand and harmonic phrase,
a whispering statue, a tree
                    in plain attire.

The (Pillow) Sham Theory

> *Only the lame stands—on*
> *three legs.*
> —William Carlos Williams, *Paterson*

1

Look at this blue brink. Look at all the little rowboats.
These hairy-backed hornets splayed out on the lake's
tethered skin. What becomes of such a parsed
and airless scene? Somewhere, there must sneer
dollops of failed parachutes atop hapless trees, an army
of green gnats, pine skulls, and piss?
A false eye cracked in a nest of needles.
A hunchbacked gnome with a stitched-up wrist.

But who am I to say? A bed-ridden bedbug.
I bask in the best ward,
half-baked-house, half-toll-.
The clinical cowhands wear wolfsuits
that unzip to yield wolves.

Down the hall, a great itch is coming on,
a pursed-lip gesture the color of hospice.
What a pity it is, what a pity indeed, some fond thing
squalls from behind the gummed glass.

I am sapped,
                    or I am sapping
Wherever I look is a dogstar laughing,
                                   an orderly's apron flapping.

These loose tendons, useless tentacles.
All my love goes undirected.

And the belfry,

the near belfry,
how it bongs.

2

At Carl Schurz Park, I am sapping lemon juice and pulp into Sarah's unwashed hair. The seeds stick to her scalp. We want everything: the rinds, the acid, the gore. *Let none of it go to waste. Let none of it think you extravagant.* On this half of the island, it is just high-noon. Or to put it starkly: I am the black rook, and she is the golden. Beyond us, what we do not realize: A harbor caves in like a highway. The damn contraption was misassembled.

There is so much nature here, it is shameful, Sarah opines.

The night before, we worked. We hacked at an unsuspecting fennel, a ham-hock, our intransigent freezer. We listened to two Argentines mimic Puerto Rican Spanish over porcelain plates. *It's the radio talking, it's the encyclopedia set ogling,* we warned each other. Sarah's ankle had buckled under from the weight of nonbeing, or the terror of happiness. Love, O love, and garlic salt streaming. It rained on us like volcanic ash. It refused to let up for hours.

3

What is wellness? Does it have a ridged snout?
Could it tell a Djindjic from a Zizic?
Say psalms for choirboys, utter prayers for the dead?

Could it thresh wheat for just a pint-sized parish?
Can it airlift an armoire, devour a door?
Can it thread quilting needles with the nib of its tongue?

Can it, if it wants to, let dear Brutus off the hook?
Turn a mirror on prudence, make a sluice from a tusk?
If not, if not, *what good is it?*

What good indeed—It is fucked straight through.
Like X to X to X.
And these slews of cherubic ol' haunters,

in the business of tenterhooks
and dying, are all believed well?
O Candystriper, sweetheart, this bedspread's got a nasty stain.

For now, even my good aunt taunts.
She nurses her headless self, her
spell-ful ill. The right eye gone dull to a piebald pellet,

her hair slips out like strings of soap. She sweats
to finish a steak. That Soviet way,
the way she learned to speak to a camera:

unmoved, like a spotted deerhead in lights.
She states the rot plainly,
she wears the gown gladly.

This dear aunt allows us witness: bell-sleeved,
patchy-handed, how she labors
over a pink bone, a scalloped plate edge

with the will of a seasoned martyr.
O how the ceiling arches over us
recessed, a cornflower blue inverted pool

whose water is sucked to an ether.
This is how we distract our longing:
A pill becomes a wand becomes

a potion becomes a cure becomes
a god. And so on this way, the dog—
it chases, chases its tail. It swallows paper prayers.

And when my aunt's gaze lifts to meet with mine,
it could damn, perhaps salute,
but all the time, it envies:

Just look at you. *To be young*—she blithely hisses—
To have reverence for nothing.

4

There but for the grace of God go a three-legged dog.

It leaps!
It leaps!
It leaps!

Sarah has fled the city and left explicit, ink-wet instructions. *Bring down the wall, cut up the phone lines. Heaven's skint. We are its heirs.* In the morning, I seem smaller than small, elfin even, just a pink dot! Left to bemoan the loss of knives, the tattered springs, an owlish kitchen. The thermometer, lifted from my tongue, reads, "Bah, bah, bah." So this is my desire. A series of chewed-up prescriptions, a litany of bells. During evaluations, another wise Ibsen-ian man dismisses me in my paper purple poncho.

You win, he starts, *you always do, by virtue of being you.*

How would you compose this shallow life? How would you have me say it? My body on a board. *My dear, darling Auntie, I just wanted you to know: The whole world smells of paraffin. The whole day smacks of dog.*

Fortuna

All July, I had an itch in my fish. Dumb hooks, chunks of salt. A traveler appeared to me from under an umbrella. His hands in tremble. In treble.

This was seven years ago. Before the pond I broke up into bite-size pieces. Before the clumps of clover I crammed in my mouth. Before the chore of coming to, the burden of morning—*dumbwaiter, anvil, stone.* Lug, lug, lug.

This was absolute middle C: moon voices, hyena voices, drones and moth-beats. The lighthouse lit at the horns. I spat from a Gothic window. Listened to the buzz of razors above.

After dinner, a Turkish fortune-teller saw a horse in the coffee dregs and told me I was happy.

In the sanctuary, my lungs whistled.

Torch Song

A rose from a tor, or
mold furs from a cup,

some morbid tire
or more piles high

on hilltop
like a tor. (Depose?)

Blood on a thorn
bars a floor.

Caught stare, blunt flaw,
a start not seen, a pinch

not cornered, like a thorn
with bud, but torn—

No gullet sought, sill
seldom mulled, like a tarp

pulled taut, all under:
heart. A whim be bought,

or word be tarred, a good
deferred, like a moor,

unstarred—A thought
goes far, though

nought be earned. Sod
returns a sod—

Hydrovulturia

How long has the vulture been sleeping?

One side of its head all jungled
and matte.
It plunges at some ripple.

Each of us starts out this way,
then shrinks back from the ledge
where the corked jars glare.

We dream of the one
we've wronged.
And pick at his elephant bones.

And the sighs of such seas,
the water
wolfs.

There,
the couple in the window:
The woman bites his fingers.

Why did you always forgive me?

Glacier

That a field of ice
does not acquiesce—

That it meets the sea
and calves
its sundered selves,

bergs. Breath
is no authority.

That there was this
glacier in me,
firn-slid,

down-slope.
And far from center.

The light rose
hungered.
And the sky in consensus:

matte drifts
and no temperature.
All this slowness.

Heaviness.
At the rate of
living—

6

Dream of Irving

Half-past blackjack in the abandoned casino,
    and all the dealers anguished.

In that tentacular, grey-eyed moment,
right after the clarinets go quiet,
the women arrive in elemental fashion:
hems of ice and hats of holly,
a little musk on the queen's left lily,
clutched in her whitish fist.

One would like to insist on surface,
on the placid faces of even numbers and dreams.
One would like to be seen
leaning against a sunlit wall
or caressing an American pearl king.
Or, to wear one's gown to the tennis court wedding
(a succession of asthmatic brides)
and mimic the vows from behind the net
while quietly peeling an orange.
    Is it sun down already, friends?

(The men intercept the mail.
    The brides play darts while melting.)

The mind perceives in everything
    a spade just out of place.

*

The trouble with Irving is boredom.
    Permanent name-tag, mismatched sideburns.

Analogy confused with *syllogism*.
Glass shard masquerading as *prism*.
You can see it this way if you want to.

Or, shut one eye and lo,
      a flattened pearl is half its worth.

Underwater, Irving remembers
long renditions of *Mother, May I? May I?*
He feels safe to voice his opinions,
      at liberty to cradle his turnip.

Knowledge comes in sea-ward flashes,
breeding schools of silent letters.

      Tortoise is to *people* as *pneumonia* is to *cupboard*.

You've heard it all before.

It's telekinetic: The glass drops off the table.
Perfumed letters afire in large aluminum buckets.
The men intercept the mail.

Are you the glass, or are you the table?
You can see it this way at last.

(How beautiful to watch
      the brides inhale en masse…)

On the tennis court, all the ball boys chant:
Arboretum. A moratorium. And the amputated arms.
Toss your rinds their way in typical vaudeville form.

Or pin down the wayward seascape with a single copper tack.

(Go back, Irving. Go back.
	The ace of clubs, the jack.)

Do you feel a strong desire for vestigial wings and terms?
Do you hear maternal voices from the missives as they burn?
"Enlarge the circle." "Relax the vigilance."
(A feedback loop of fantasies.)

Underwater, you confess to fainting. *I feel a little degraded*
	in the shoes of other feet.
Meanwhile, on the ocean floor, a mammalian shadow creeps.

And the brides play darts while melting
a hemline at a time. *O Frieda, Penny, Eleanor…*
	careful where you step.

You light a big cigar, you speak in stentorian manner.
You glimpse in the mist a pair of faces,
	but long for the one that is farther.

Dream of Sabine

If this is so, then *so.*
Go to the thinking corner,
in one hand a sandwich, the other a horn, he said.
Smashing, Sabine

thought. And when she was done, she thought
still more & again, even so much as
besides which but *exactly.*
The plague was on her. A rabid dog.

Sooner or later, the itching in her throat took
to itching her hand. This horn, & what for?
She looked to friends: *One of you's got my trigger
happy.* The TV snapped black, just

off. A newsy conclusion was ready.
"I have a little bit, an announcement," she teared up
all Canadian-like.
At the end of the spit was the pig she roasted:

To be able to say, *This is not mine,*
to muffle this petty horn against a petty wall—

*

So much to do, she said. Nutting.
And to finish the knitting. To learn to say maybe
in thirteen different far-off tongues.
But a melancholic is easily swayed from such

bull's-eyes. This one, she burrowed often.
You'll find me like a wet wad
in a furred place. All told, death is a hard
hugger. His hairy arms a rope.

This winter was a war toward slow-
motion, toward
a distant gray feathering. The firs still bristling with pod
& opinion. So little happens that we can praise,

she felt, her body plumb stuck.
When things get bad, will you pray for nuttin'?
Those almond trees popped: *Maybe, maybe, maybe.*
Or such brittle hope, when it was.

Dream of the Birds

Live needlers of
skulls and kneecaps
prick these human shapes,

incessant, they
invite their beaks
to horn in, to snap

pole-wires so voices
skip or pine, all
static gauze, replace

an ease, all gummous
plants endure the fowl
arrival. This

black crowd that makes
intent its arch-
itecture, by flock-

instinct, it, flanking,
forms a silhouette.
However gutted,

however spent,
cawing a town in
fanatic wager,

as two green lovebirds
sway—a synchronous
set, not accomplice,

not alighting—
what crude nature
routs this way? What

dim desire coils
here, unravels us
with beckoning?

Dream of Mae West

Mores change. Overgrown gardens too
change, go further over, hundreds of laden bushes:
peonies place their layered
heads on the ground to manage their overweight.
And on her 71st birthday, Mae West feasts on cake
studded with rhinestones. She has outlasted
every suited suitor
or pasty local lover, exhausted
profusions of pastel diamonds, she has gone over
her own nude likeness, greatly impersonating
the greatest female impersonation
the world over—

Each night she is presented with a choice:
a round bed or a square one.
Better yet, there is a subtle
fidelity about her: In the kitchen pantry
wearing apricot-peach satin & lipstick, she consults
her butler. "You know how it is."
Her monkeys adore her. Seas change,
mores change. Idolatry begins at the first act of touching
the idol's pale hem. Gentlemen come up to the gold villa
and sometimes sugared blossoms,
brushed over by wind, lift their heads just to nod
a brief nod.

How to Take Black-and-White Pictures

1

Imagine a painted door. Owl eyes. A tiny blue egg
arranged on a ladder with other birds' eggs.
Rat bells, as in, *You hear rat bells all along the wall.*
It helps you. You get some sleep in the bathtub,
draw a horse-head with a soapy finger. It dissolves. Two sun streaks.
You are the maid-of-honor, you are the private equestrian.
What you like. Rained-out appointments. A tall carafe.
Card-games and hand-me-down sweaters.
Imagine a house packed with jacks. Dishes piled, a man-servant.
Snapshot. Your last journal entry reads: *The Last Supper.*
It wakes you. You want a floor to drag a doll over.
An armoire. A barrel of tar. The heaviest thing will do.

2

Imagine owl eyes, all along the wall. A colored egg
hidden in the fireplace. A sunburn. You step into a painted hole.
Mothballs, as in, *A bee-shaped jewel you keep in mothballs.*
It alarms you. You get some sleep in the dentist's chair, dream
of a pair of saints. They drag their feet. Two ice-cubes.
You are the state senator, you are the private doll-maker.
What you like. Apothecaries. Seven-layer cakes.
A set of flattened spoons. It helps you.
Imagine a fur shop packed with rats. A window dressing. An itch.
You switch cameras. Your first journal entry reads:
Found a frozen blue jay on the front step today. It reminds you.
You want a sea to toss sandbags over. A door-stop
of cat's-eye marbles. A dead motor. The steadiest thing will do.

How to Make Bells

Maybe it is the epoch of strange jesters, their faces caked in make-up. A cortege of chewed plum pits placed across the table. You don't ask. You erase a part of the recording by mistake. You get chased. You still get distracted by these engravings of toothless saints, haloed in sulfur and pith.

You wake up every morning reciting the three holy virtues. Or they recite you. It doesn't matter. Your search for clay isn't discouraged by a sudden rainstorm. You keep on, hunting for a particular stain and the scent of hailstone, something that can slide off metal. You think, *This will be the mold that holds it, this will be the matter.*

Steeped in a pool of red light, one of your horses rolls over and struggles to stand. It steadies itself. It gallops off the frame. Then the reel repeats. *Faith.* You concentrate on the fricative. You remember how you got here.

NOTES

On "Articles of Faith": In Mormonism, there are thirteen articles of faith, several of which children are strongly encouraged to memorize before reaching adolescence. The articles concisely summarize the main tenets of the church, including, as stated in Article Four, "We believe that the first principles and ordinances of the Gospel are: first, Faith in the Lord Jesus Christ; second, Repentance; third, Baptism by immersion for the remission of sins; fourth, Laying on of hands for the gift of the Holy Ghost."

The "Minority Assignment" poems are inspired by a 1985-86 Martin Kippenberger exhibition: *"Was ist ihre Lieblingsminderheit? Wen beneiden Sie am meisten?" (Which is your favorite minority? Who do you envy the most?)*

"Minority Assignment #7" is a partially found poem with the word "minority" replacing various nouns. The found fragments were taken from Ludwig Wittgenstein's *The Blue and Brown Books* and Krome Barratt's *Logic and Design*.

"Stage Notes for *Clay Winter Wedding*" is in homage to Carl Wildman and Jean Cocteau.

"Dream of the Birds" is after Alfred Hitchcock's 1963 film, "The Birds."

"How to Take Black-and-White Pictures": The last entry of Diane Arbus' diary reads, "The Last Supper."

"How to Make Bells" refers in parts to Andrei Tarkovsky's film *Andrei Rublev*.

Also Available from saturnalia books:

Ladies & Gentlemen by Michael Robins

Other Romes by Derek Mong

Faulkner's Rosary by Sarah Vap

Gurlesque: the new grrly, grotesque, burlesque poetics edited by Lara Glenum and
Arielle Greenberg

Tsim Tsum by Sabrina Orah Mark

Hush Sessions by Kristi Maxwell

Days of Unwilling by Cal Bedient

Letters to Poets: Conversations about Poetics, Politics, and Community
edited by Jennifer Firestone and Dana Teen Lomax

The Little Office of the Immaculate Conception by Martha Silano
Winner of the Saturnalia Books Poetry Prize 2010

Personification by Margaret Ronda
Winner of the Saturnalia Books Poetry Prize 2009

To the Bone by Sebastian Agudelo
Winner of the Saturnalia Books Poetry Prize 2008

Famous Last Words by Catherine Pierce
Winner of the Saturnalia Books Poetry Prize 2007

Dummy Fire by Sarah Vap
Winner of the Saturnalia Books Poetry Prize 2006

Correspondence by Kathleen Graber
Winner of the Saturnalia Books Poetry Prize 2005

The Babies by Sabrina Orah Mark
Winner of the Saturnalia Books Poetry Prize 2004

Velleity's Shade by Star Black / Artwork by Bill Knott

Polytheogamy by Timothy Liu / Artwork by Greg Drasler

Midnights by Jane Miller / Artwork by Beverly Pepper

Stigmata Errata Etcetera by Bill Knott / Artwork by Star Black

Ing Grish by John Yau / Artwork by Thomas Nozkowski

Blackboards by Tomaz Salamun / Artwork by Metka Krasovec

Xing was printed using the fonts Futura and Baskerville.

www.saturnaliabooks.org